SAGE'S SHOOTERS:

The Original Gelatin Shooter Recipe Book

Laurie Sage Morris

American Literary Press, Inc.
Five Star Special Edition
Baltimore, Maryland

Sage's Shooters:
The Original Gelatin Shooter Recipe Book

Copyright © 1995 Laurie Sage Morris

The Surgeon General warns that alcoholic consumption may be detrimental to the health of an unborn fetus, may seriously impair one's ability to operate heavy machinery or drive a motor vehicle, and may cause health problems.

Library of Congress
Cataloging in Publication Data
ISBN 1-56167-237-8
Library of Congress Card Catalog Number:
95-083133

Published by

American Literary Press, Inc.
Five Star Special Edition
8019 Belair Road, Suite 10
Baltimore, Maryland 21236

Manufactured in the United States of America

DEDICATION

This book is dedicated with great appreciation to the Outer Banks "Beach People" who help me celebrate life on all occasions.   You know who you are, and you'll see most of your favorite shooters listed here in your honor!

2

Table of Contents

INTRODUCTION

"Gello-Shooters." Yes, you have all heard of them, "done them," and even a few of you have attempted to make them. Well, finally here is a recipe book that will tell you exactly how to make them and also give you ideas on the many combinations that make gelatin-shooters one of the most popular party favors today!

No one seems to know who invented gelatin-shooters. I doubt it was Bill Cosby, but who knows! My first experience with them occurred at a small hotel bar in Virginia. A bartender, who I'll call Petty (Larsen is her last name), gave me one and it was delicious - since then it's been history! Petty told me the basic recipe and where to find the cups to put them in. Since then, I've experimented with various recipes and holiday combinations. When people invite me to parties, they always ask me to "bring your shooters", and depending on the occasion I vary the colors and flavors.

In this book you will find: the basic "Gelatin-Shooter" recipe, lots of recipe combinations, and a section on various party suggestions. Good luck and be brave - make up your own combination with your favorite liquors!

HOW TO EAT A GELATIN-SHOOTER

There are two methods of eating a shooter.

First Method

Open the cup. Insert your tongue firmly down between the side of the cup and the gelatin itself. Move your tongue (seductively, if you wish!) around the cup by rotating the cup with your hand, letting your tongue loosen the entire piece of gelatin. Once you feel that the gelatin is completely free, withdraw your tongue and suck the gelatin out of the cup! Present the empty cup to the air as a toast with a triumphant look in your eyes! You may optionally slam-dunk the empty cup into a trash receptacle.

Second Method

Open the cup. Insert your finger between the side of the cup and the gelatin itself. Move your finger around the cup, letting your finger loosen the entire piece of gelatin. Once you feel that the gelatin is free, withdraw your finger and suck the gelatin out of the cup! Present the empty cup to the air as a toast with a triumphant look in your eyes, and a slight blush to show that you are the shy, reserved type.

7

BASIC GELATIN-SHOOTER RECIPE

Tools:

2-ounce plastic cups and lids
2 or 4-cup Glass/Pyrex Measuring Cup
Spoon
Water
Various Liquors
3-ounce box of gelatin mix (both sugar and sugar-free work)

Recipe:

Microwave or heat 1 cup water to boiling. (I generally use the glass measuring cup for this and do all of my mixing and pouring from the same item.) Mix together boiling water with the box of flavored gelatin. Stir until dissolved - usually about two minutes. Instead of the usual cup cold water that follows, mix in a cup liquor. This is the secret of gelatin-shooters!

Got it? Hot water.....Gelatin.....Liquor!

Now, pour mixture into the 2 ounce cups - generally you would want to fill the cups half-full (i.e. one ounce of shooter per cup). That way you make about 16 shooters.

9

Put the lids on each cup and put them in the refrigerator for at least three hours.

Note: DO NOT try to add *more* liquor than 1 cup - too much liquid (water or liquor) will cause the gelatin not to get firm. (Do not pass Go, do not collect two hundred dollars!).

Pop the lids and try one, they're delicious!

Due to the large number of shooter flavors, the recipes are listed alphabetically! Note, you can always make VIRGIN gelatin-shooters for those friends of yours that are pregnant, designated drivers, non-drinkers, etc. that want to eat gelatin-shooters with the rest of the gang but do not want or need the alcohol. Look under "V" for this one!

A's and B's (ABSOLUT-LY the BEST)

Alice in Wonderland
(now that book was definitely written by someone eating gelatin-shooters........)

Add strawberry gelatin mix to 1 cup boiling water.   Mix well.

Add the following liquors:
* 1/3 cup Absolut Vodka
* 1/3 cup Midori
* 1/3 cup Peach Schnapps

Angler

Add orange gelatin mix to 1 cup boiling water. Mix well.

Add the following liquors:
* 1/2 cup Rum
* 1/2 cup Peach Schnapps

(This is also well known as a red-headed freckle-faced man-catcher, right Sarah?)

11

Apple Jack

Add cherry gelatin mix to 1 cup boiling water. Mix well.

Add the following liquors:
- 1/3 cup Jack Daniel's
- 1/3 cup Apple Brandy
- 1/3 cup Peach Schnapps

Apricot Anise

Add strawberry-banana gelatin mix to 1 cup boiling water.   Mix well.

Add the following liquors:
- 1/2 cup Gin
- 1/4 cup Apricot Brandy
- 1/4 cup Anisette

Atlanta Joe's Snakebite

Add lime gelatin mix to 1 cup boiling water. Mix well.

Add the following liquors:
- 1/2 cup Wild Turkey
- 1/4 cup Orange Curacao
- 1/4 cup Peppermint Schnapps

B-I-N-G-O

Add strawberry-banana gelatin mix to 1 cup boiling water.   Mix well.

Add the following liquors:
- 1/5 cup Banana Liqueur
- 1/5 cup Irish Whiskey
- 1/5 cup Nice Rum
  (this is any rum that you think is "nice")
- 1/5 cup Gin
- 1/5 cup Orange Liqueur

Baby Maker
(for Cindy and the girls...)

Add cherry gelatin mix to 1 cup boiling water. Mix well.

Add the following liquors:
- 1/2 cup Vodka
- 1/4 cup Raspberry Schnapps
- 1/4 cup Triple Sec

(this shooter is guaranteed to make you want to jump in the sack!)

13

Bahama Mama
(Favorite of Kathie's - aka "mom")

Add Hawaiian-pineapple gelatin mix to 1 cup boiling water.   Mix well.

Add the following liquors:
- 1/2 cup Coconut Rum
- 1/4 cup Peach Schnapps
- 1/4 cup Triple Sec

Banana Split

Add strawberry-banana gelatin mix to 1 cup boiling water.   Mix well.

Add the following liquors:
- 1/2 cup Banana Liqueur
- 1/4 cup Frangelico
- 1/4 cup Butterscotch Schnapps

Beachcomber

Add lime gelatin mix to 1 cup boiling water. Mix well.

Add the following liquors:
- 1/3 cup Rum
- 1/3 cup Triple Sec
- 1/3 cup Cherry Liqueur

Belly-Button-Gelatin-Shooter

Step 1:   Add any gelatin-shooter (removed from cup with method #2) to any persons belly button (they should be lying down for this).

Step 2:   Any other person can then suck the shooter off of the lie-ee's belly-button.

Note, the shooter is **cold** so when placing the gelatin-shooter on the belly-button, watch out as the lie-ee may jump suddenly hitting the shooter-placer in the head.

Bermuda High

Add orange gelatin mix to 1 cup boiling water. Mix well.

Add the following liquors:
- 1/2 cup Gin
- 1/4 cup Apricot Brandy
- 1/4 cup Peach Schnapps

Between the Sheets

Add lemon gelatin mix to 1 cup boiling water.
Mix well.

Add the following liquors:
- 1/3 cup Cointreau
- 1/3 cup Rum
- 1/3 cup Brandy

Black Beauty

Add grape gelatin mix to 1 cup boiling water.
Mix well.

Add the following liquors:
- 1/2 cup Blackberry liqueur or Schnapps
- 1/2 cup Blackberry Brandy

Black Russian in Red Square

Add cherry gelatin mix to 1 cup boiling water.
Mix well.

Add the following liquors:
- 1/2 cup Kahlua
- 1/2 cup Vodka

Blow Job

(this is fun to serve at bachelor and bachelorette parties!!)

Step 1:   Take any already gelled gelatin-shooter and remove the lid.   Pre-loosen the shooter by running a finger around the sides of the shooter (inside the cup!).

Step 2:   Put a dab of whipped cream on the shooter and place it on a table or flat surface.

Step 3:   The person eating the shooter must first place both hands behind his/her back.

Step 4:   The person should then put their mouth around the shooter and attempt to suck it in and eat it all in one action.

Step 5: To successfully have completed this shooter, the person needs to swallow the whole thing.

(Steady, now.......)

Blue Hawaii

Add blueberry gelatin mix to 1 cup boiling water.   Mix well.

Add the following liquors:
- 1/2 cup Light Rum
- 1/4 cup Blue Curacao
- 1/4 cup Blueberry Schnapps

BOOP
(for Sue who got Booped more than most!)
Add cherry gelatin mix to 1 cup boiling water. Mix well.

Add the following liquors:
- 1/2 cup Citron Vodka
- 1/2 cup Cherry Brandy

Brigand
(aka a Pirate - Brussels American High School mascot.   Class of '76, where are you??!!!)
Add blueberry gelatin mix to 1 cup boiling water.   Mix well.

Add the following liquors:
- 1/2 cup Coconut Rum
- 1/4 cup Dark Rum
- 1/4 cup Banana Liqueur

Bubba's Batch

Add watermelon gelatin mix to 1 cup boiling water.   Mix well.

Add the following liquors:
- 1/3 cup Banana Liqueur
- 1/3 cup Peach Schnapps
- 1/3 cup Vodka

"Bubba-licious!"

Bull Horns

Add cherry gelatin mix to 1 cup boiling water. Mix well.

Add the following liquors:
- 1/2 cup Tequila
- 1/2 cup Kahlua

Buster Cherry

Add cherry gelatin mix to 1 cup boiling water. Mix well.

Add the following liquors:
- 1/2 cup Cherry Brandy
- 1/2 cup Rum

C's and D's (no, NOT Cats and Dogs)

Candy Cane
(Layer two colors by using the second method of shooter removal, and putting a dab of whipped cream in between the two before serving thus getting the striped look!)

Add cherry gelatin mix to 1 cup boiling water. Mix well.

Add the following liquors:
- 3/4 cup Peppermint Schnapps
- 1/4 cup Vodka

Warning, this may bring about unexpected Christmas Cheer!!

Cape Codder

Add Cranberry gelatin mix to 1 cup boiling water. Mix well.

Add the following liquors:
- 1/2 cup Vodka
- 1/4 cup Triple Sec
- 1/4 cup Cranberry Liqueur

Go North, young man!!

Caribbean Cocktail

Add Hawaiian-pineapple gelatin mix to 1 cup boiling water. Mix well.

Add the following liquors:
- 1/2 cup White Rum
- 1/2 cup Midori

Carolina Blues
(when you're not in the Outer Banks, this is what you have)

Add blueberry gelatin mix to 1 cup boiling water. Mix well.

Add the following liquors:
- 1/4 cup Rum
- 1/4 cup Chambord
- 1/2 cup Blueberry Schnapps

Catty Women
(any explanation needed?)

Add cherry gelatin mix to 1 cup boiling water. Mix well.

Add the following liquors:
- 1/2 cup Dark Rum
- 1/2 cup Blue Curacao

Check-Bouncer   (Petty's favorite!)

Add cherry gelatin mix to 1 cup boiling water. Mix well.

Add the following liquors:
- 1/2 cup Grand Marnier
- 1/2 cup Tequila

(not in MY checkbook, you don't!)

Christmas Tree

Add lime gelatin mix to 1 cup boiling water. Mix well.

Add the following liquors:
- 1/2 cup Goldwasser
- 1/2 cup Peach Schnapps

(this shooter will have little specs of gold floating in it due to the Goldwasser - Cool!)

Coconut Brandy

Add Hawaiian-pineapple gelatin mix to 1 cup boiling water.   Mix well.

Add the following liquors:
- 1/2 cup Coconut Rum
- 1/2 cup Apricot Brandy

23

Divorce Club
(*or the second-time around club!*)

Add raspberry gelatin mix to 1 cup boiling water.   Mix well.

Add the following liquors:
- 1/4 cup Rum
- 1/4 cup Vodka
- 1/4 cup Tequila
- 1/4 cup Cinnamon Schnapps

"Three's a charm" for some!

The Doctor
(*don't try this at home, call a professional - like Ed - "it won't hurt a bit......"*)

Add lime gelatin mix to 1 cup boiling water. Mix well.

Add the following liquors:
- 1/2 cup Dark Rum
- 1/4 cup Triple Sec
- 1/4 cup Cinnamon Schnapps

Double-Trouble
(for all the TWINs I know)

Add lime gelatin mix to 1 cup boiling water.
Mix well.

Add the following liquors:
- 1/2 cup Tequila
- 1/4 cup Cinnamon Schnapps
- 1/4 cup Coconut Rum

Drag Race

Add any red gelatin mix to 1 cup boiling
water. Mix well.

Add the following liquors:
- 1/2 cup Jack Daniel's
- 1/2 cup Berry Liqueur or Schnapps

Dragon Fire

Add lime gelatin mix to 1 cup boiling water.
Mix well.

Add the following liquors:
- 1/2 cup Pepper Vodka
- 1/2 cup Peppermint Schnapps

Add a dash of Tabasco for extra kick!

E's, F's, and G's   (EASY FOR GIRLS)

Early Bird

Add orange gelatin mix to 1 cup boiling water.
Mix well.

Add the following liquors:
- 1/2 cup Tequila
- 1/2 cup Peppermint Schnapps
- optional: worm from the tequila!!

East Coast

Add watermelon gelatin mix to 1 cup boiling
water.   Mix well.

Add the following liquors:
- 1/2 cup Gin
- 1/2 cup Cherry or Raspberry Liqueur

Easy Street
(hopefully after writing a book...??)

Add strawberry gelatin mix to 1 cup boiling
water.   Mix well.

Add the following liquors:
- 1/2 cup Berry Vodka
- 1/2 cup Banana Liqueur

27

Fireball

Add cherry gelatin mix to 1 cup boiling water. Mix well.

Add the following liquors:
- 1/4 cup Pepper Vodka
- 3/4 cup Cinnamon Schnapps

(you might need a chaser after this one!)

Firemen

Add Cranberry gelatin mix to 1 cup boiling water.   Mix well.

Add the following liquors:
- 1/2 cup Gin
- 1/2 cup Cherry Brandy

Flaming A
(for the Telenet Softball League)

Add lime gelatin mix to 1 cup boiling water. Mix well.

Add the following liquors:
- 1/2 cup Triple Sec
- 1/2 cup Peppermint Schnapps

Frankenstein

Add cherry gelatin mix to 1 cup boiling water. Mix well.

Add the following liquors:
- 1/2 cup Gin
- 1/2 cup Orange Curacao

French Connection
(for all of us working for "The French Company")

Add mixed fruit gelatin mix to 1 cup boiling water. Mix well.

Add the following liquors:
- 1/2 cup Chambord
- 1/4 cup Triple Sec
- 1/4 cup Anisette

Fuzzy Navels
(these also make good belly-button shooters!)
Add orange gelatin mix to 1 cup boiling water. Mix well.

Add the following liquors:
- 1/2 cup Vodka
- 1/2 cup Peach Schnapps

Georgia Peach
(aka: Colleen-does-Atlanta)

Add Hawaiian-pineapple gelatin mix to 1 cup boiling water.   Mix well.

Add the following liquors:
- 1/2 cup Peach Brandy
- 1/2 cup Peach Schnapps

Gimlet

Add lime gelatin mix to 1 cup boiling water. Mix well.

Add the following liquor:
- Full cup Citron Vodka

Gin-Rummy

Add grape gelatin mix to 1 cup boiling water. Mix well.

Add the following liquors:
- 1/3 cup Gin
- 1/3 cup Rum
- 1/3 cup Banana Liqueur

Golden Years

Add orange gelatin mix to 1 cup boiling water. Mix well.

Add the following liquors:
- 1/2 cup Goldwasser
- 1/2 cup Vodka

This will send you back a few!

Grand-E-Orange

Add orange gelatin mix to 1 cup boiling water. Mix well.

Add the following liquors:
- 1/2 cup Grand Marnier
- 1/2 cup Triple Sec

Grape Vines

Add grape gelatin mix to 1 cup boiling water. Mix well.

Add the following liquors:
- 1/2 cup Rum
- 1/2 cup Blueberry Schnapps

Grasshopper

Add lime gelatin mix to 1 cup boiling water.
Mix well.

Add the following liquors:
- 1/2 cup Gin
- 1/2 cup Peppermint Schnapps

Grog

Add lemon gelatin mix to 1 cup boiling water.
Mix well.

Add the following liquors:
- 1/2 cup Jamaican Rum
- 1/4 cup Cinnamon Schnapps
- 1/4 cup Peach Schnapps

H's, I's, J's, K's (ELOPING IS PEAK)

Hatteras High
(this light house provides a great romantic spot for engagements, sex, or just gazing into loved-ones eyes......)

Add cherry gelatin mix to 1 cup boiling water. Mix well.

Add the following liquors:
- 1/4 cup Dark Rum
- 1/4 cup Gin
- 1/2 cup Amaretto

Havana
(or have any of us, for that matter!)

Add lemon gelatin mix to 1 cup boiling water. Mix well.

Add the following liquors:
- 1/4 cup Apricot Brandy
- 1/4 cup any Berry Schnapps
- 1/2 cup Gin

(You can carry these through Customs - unlike Mr. Ryan's cigars!!)

Hindsight
(if only we knew then what we know now......)

Add mixed fruit gelatin mix to 1 cup boiling water.   Mix well.

Add the following liquors:
- 1/4 cup Vodka
- 1/4 cup Gin
- 1/2 cup   Banana Liqueur

Hokie-Pokey
For all those Virginia Tech Fans!
"you put your index finger in,
to pull the shooter out,
you run your finger right around
......................and you shake it all about!"

Add orange gelatin mix to 1 cup boiling water. Mix well.

Add the following liquors:
- 1/2 cup Triple Sec
- 1/4 cup Vodka
- 1/4 cup Peppermint Schnapps

(be careful on the "shake it all about" part - you may become one of the   "Hurl Girls"!)

Hurl Girls
(especially for Kathie, Chris, and Carol)

Add strawberry-banana gelatin mix to 1 cup boiling water. Mix well.

Add the following liquors:
- 1/3 cup Tequila
- 1/3 cup Raspberry Liqueur
- 1/3 cup Peach Schnapps

(eat these prior to going to The DUNES..)

Hurricane

Add Hawaiian-pineapple gelatin mix to 1 cup boiling water. Mix well.

Add the following liquors:
- 1/3 cup Outer Banks Rum (white)
- 1/3 cup Gold Rum
- 1/3 cup Peach Schnapps

Andrew, Emily, Felix and Hugo love this one!!

35

Hustle (as in "Do the....")

Add orange gelatin mix to 1 cup boiling water. Mix well.

Add the following liquors:
- 1/2 cup Bourbon
- 1/2 cup Orange Curacao

I.D.H. ("I'd Do Him/Her!")

Add cherry gelatin mix to 1 cup boiling water. Mix well.

Add the following liquors:
- 1/4 cup Gin
- 1/4 cup Rum
- 1/2 cup Cinnamon Schnapps

Injection

Add grape gelatin mix to 1 cup boiling water. Mix well.

Add the following liquors:
- 1/3 cup Vodka
- 1/3 cup Rum
- 1/3 cup Peppermint Schnapps

Jamaican Dust
(also known as Hedonism II - call Pam, Patty, Rose or me for details!)

Add Hawaiian-pineapple gelatin mix to 1 cup boiling water.   Mix well.

Add the following liquors:
- 1/3 cup Tia Maria
- 2/3 cup Light Rum

Jelly-Bean

Add raspberry gelatin mix to 1 cup boiling water.   Mix well.

Add the following liquors:
- 1/3 cup Blackberry Brandy
- 1/3 cup Southern Comfort
- 1/3 cup Chambord (or berry liqueur)

Jelly-Bean #2 (Licorice)

Add grape gelatin mix to 1 cup boiling water. Mix well.

Add the following liquors:
- 2/3 cup Sambuca
- 1/3 cup Citron Vodka

Johnny Cocktail
(very popular in St.Louis)

Add Cranberry gelatin mix to 1 cup boiling water. Mix well.

Add the following liquors:
- 1/3 cup Sloe gin
- 1/3 cup Orange Curacao
- 1/3 cup Anisette

Joker (just joe-king!)

Add strawberry gelatin mix to 1 cup boiling water. Mix well.

Add the following liquors:
- 1/4 cup Vodka
- 1/4 cup Southern Comfort
- 1/2 cup Tequila

Jones Dorm
(for the "motel girls" at Randolph-Macon College!! Still Crazy after all these years!!!)

Add orange gelatin mix to 1 cup boiling water. Mix well.

Add the following liquors:
- 3/4 cup Tequila
- 1/4 cup any other liquor!

Kamikaze
(the real shooters can often be found under tables in bars as they are generally difficult to drink!)

Add lime gelatin mix to 1 cup boiling water. Mix well.

Add the following liquors:
- 1/2 cup Vodka
- 1/4 cup Triple Sec
- 1/4 cup Peppermint Schnapps

Kentucky Derby

Add orange gelatin mix to 1 cup boiling water. Mix well.

Add the following liquors:
- 1/2 cup Bourbon
- 1/2 cup Triple Sec

Bring these to any horse races, point-to-points, or steeple chases!! (If you lose your shirt on betting, you won't even notice.)

Key Lime Pie

Add lime gelatin mix to 1 cup boiling water.
Mix well.

Add the following liquors:
* 1/2 cup Vodka
* 1/2 cup Triple Sec
* dab of whipped cream

Key West
(New Year's Eve - 1999 - Be there!!)

Add lime gelatin mix to 1 cup boiling water.
Mix well.

Add the following liquors:
* 1/2 cup Gin
* 1/4 cup Banana Liqueur
* 1/4 cup Triple Sec

Kiss-and-Tell

Add cherry gelatin mix to 1 cup boiling water.
Mix well.

Add the following liquors:
* 1/2 cup Tequila
* 1/2 cup Peach Schnapps

L, M, N, O (REMEMBER THE ALAMO?)

Lady Finger

Add cherry gelatin mix to 1 cup boiling water. Mix well.

Add the following liquors:
- 1/3 cup Cherry Brandy
- 1/3 cup Cherry Liqueur
- 1/3 cup Gin

Lemon Drop

Add lemon gelatin mix to 1 cup boiling water. Mix well.

Add the following liquors:
- 2/3 cup Citron Vodka
- 1/3 cup Triple Sec

Light House

Add lemon gelatin mix to 1 cup boiling water. Mix well.

Add the following liquors:
- 1/2 cup Goldwasser
- 1/4 cup Citron Vodka
- 1/4 cup Triple Sec

Magic Man   (for Merc!)

Add grape gelatin mix to 1 cup boiling water. Mix well.

Add the following liquors:
- 1/2 cup Peach Schnapps
- 1/4 cup 151 Rum
- 1/4 cup Light Rum

Mai-Tai

Add mixed fruit gelatin mix to 1 cup boiling water.   Mix well.

Add the following liquors:
- 1/2 cup Gin
- 1/4 cup Triple Sec
- 1/4 cup Frangelico

(MY, what a big TIE you have........or are you just happy to see me?)

Margarita!

Add lime gelatin mix to 1 cup boiling water. Mix well.

Add the following liquors:
- 2/3 cup Tequila
- 1/3 cup Triple Sec

Maui Cocktail

Add Hawaiian-pineapple gelatin mix to 1 cup boiling water.   Mix well.

Add the following liquors:
- 1/2 cup Vodka
- 1/2 cup Banana Liqueur

Melon Ball

Add watermelon gelatin mix to 1 cup boiling water.   Mix well.

Add the following liquors:
- 2/3 cup Vodka
- 1/3 cup Midori (or melon liqueur)

M.O.A.   (Mike's of America)

Add grape gelatin mix to 1 cup boiling water. Mix well.

Add the following liquors:
- 1/2 cup Tequila
- 1/2 cup Raspberry Liqueur

Cindy   got tattooed in club initiation - watch out for this one!

Monster MASH

Add raspberry gelatin mix to 1 cup boiling water.   Mix well.

Add the following liquors:
- 2/3 cup Vodka
- 1/3 cup Triple Sec

(after MOA, Cindy had to marry MASH!)

Myrtle Beacher
(The start of the beach trips!)

Add strawberry gelatin mix to 1 cup boiling water.   Mix well.

Add the following liquors:
- 2/3 cup 151 Rum
- 1/3 cup Banana Liqueur

Navy Blues

Add blueberry gelatin mix to 1 cup boiling water.   Mix well.

Add the following liquors:
- 1/2 cup Dark Rum
- 1/4 cup Blueberry Schnapps
- 1/4 cup Blackberry Brandy

Nutty Buddy

Add raspberry gelatin mix to 1 cup boiling water.   Mix well.

Add the following liquors:
- 2/3 cup Frangelico
- 1/3 cup Praline Liqueur

Ohio-High
(Mark's Lark in the state!)

Add grape gelatin mix to 1 cup boiling water. Mix well.

Add the following liquors:
- 1/2 cup Blue Curacao
- 1/4 cup Bourbon
- 1/4 cup Peach Schnapps

Orioles (as in Baltimore)

Add orange gelatin mix to 1 cup boiling water. Mix well.

Add the following liquors:
- 1/2 cup Citron Vodka
- 1/2 cup Orange Curacao

Orgasm

Add orange gelatin mix to 1 cup boiling water. Mix well.

Add the following liquors:
- 1/3 cup Vodka
- 1/3 cup Amaretto Di Saronno
- 1/3 cup Kahlua

Outer Banks Buck

Add Strawberry-banana gelatin mix to 1 cup boiling water. Mix well.

Add the following liquors:
- 1/2 cup Banana Liqueur
- 1/2 cup Outer Banks Rum

Outlaws
(these are usually taken to County Softball games and picnics)

Add cherry gelatin mix to 1 cup boiling water. Mix well.

Add the following liquors:
- 1/2 cup Rum
- 1/4 cup Cherry Brandy
- 1/4 cup Cinnamon Schnapps

P's   ("Not in my car, you don't!")

Paco's Punch
(Deck-Jumping with Paco is a "must")
Add watermelon gelatin mix to 1 cup boiling water.   Mix well.

Add the following liquors:
- 1/2 cup Tequila
- 1/2 cup Peach Schnapps

ParaCHute

Add cherry gelatin mix to 1 cup boiling water. Mix well.

Add the following liquors:
- 1/2 cup Cherry Liqueur
- 1/2 cup Cherry Brandy

Paradise   (....or pair of dice!!)

Add Hawaiian-pineapple gelatin mix to 1 cup boiling water.   Mix well.

Add the following liquors:
- 1/2 cup Gin
- 1/4 cup Apricot Brandy
- 1/4 cup Peach Schnapps

Peaceful Easy Feeling

Add raspberry gelatin mix to 1 cup boiling water. Mix well.

Add the following liquors:
- 1/4 cup Light Rum
- 1/4 cup Dark Rum
- 1/4 cup Coconut Rum
- 1/4 cup Peach Schnapps

Peach Daiquiri

Add lemon gelatin mix to 1 cup boiling water. Mix well.

Add the following liquors:
- 1/3 cup Peach Brandy
- 1/3 cup Light Rum
- 1/3 cup Peach Schnapps

Pick-me-up
(Joe's theme song.....)

Add blueberry gelatin mix to 1 cup boiling water. Mix well.

Add the following liquors:
- 1/2 cup Berry Vodka
- 1/4 cup Anisette
- 1/4 cup Peach Schnapps

Piña Colada

Add Hawaiian-pineapple gelatin mix to 1 cup boiling water. Mix well.

Add the following liquors:
- 1/2 cup Coconut Rum
- 1/2 cup Banana Liqueur

Piñata

Add Strawberry-banana gelatin mix to 1 cup boiling water. Mix well.

Add the following liquors:
- 1/3 cup Tequila
- 1/3 cup Triple Sec
- 1/3 cup Banana Liqueur

Pink Lemonade

Add lemon gelatin mix to 1 cup boiling water. Mix well.

Add the following liquors:
- 1/4 cup Citron Vodka
- 1/4 cup Gin
- 1/4 cup Light Rum
- 1/4 cup Cranberry Liqueur

Pink Velvet

Add raspberry gelatin mix to 1 cup boiling water. Mix well.

Add the following liquors:
- 3/4 cup Vodka
- 1/4 cup Cranberry Liqueur

Planter's Punch

Add mixed fruit gelatin mix to 1 cup boiling water. Mix well.

Add the following liquors:
- 1/2 cup Rum
- 1/2 cup Triple Sec

PMS

Add Cranberry gelatin mix to 1 cup boiling water. Mix well.

Add the following liquors:
- 1/4 cup Vodka
- 1/4 cup Chambord
- 1/4 cup Raspberry Schnapps
- 1/4 cup Cranberry Liqueur

Prairie Fire

Add orange gelatin mix to 1 cup boiling water. Mix well.

Add the following liquors:
- 1/2 cup Tequila
- 1/2 cup Cinnamon Schnapps

Prairie Fire Starter

Add orange gelatin mix to 1 cup boiling water. Mix well.

Add the following liquors:
- 1/2 cup Pepper Vodka
- 1/4 cup Cinnamon Schnapps
- 1/4 cup Peppermint Schnapps

Purple-People-Eater

Add grape gelatin mix to 1 cup boiling water. Mix well.

Add the following liquors:
- 1/2 cup Gin
- 1/4 cup Cherry Liqueur
- 1/4 cup Blueberry Schnapps

Q, R, S (AS OPPOSED TO IRS) and TEEs

Queasy Street

Add watermelon gelatin mix to 1 cup boiling water.   Mix well.

Add the following liquors:
- 1/2 cup Jack Daniel's
- 1/4 cup Orange Curacao
- 1/4 cup Peach Schnapps

Quantum Leap

Add strawberry gelatin mix to 1 cup boiling water.   Mix well.

Add the following liquors:
- 1/2 cup Cointreau
- 1/2 cup Wild Turkey

Red Lion
(Lions, and Tigers, and Bears, oh MY!)

Add cherry gelatin mix to 1 cup boiling water. Mix well.

Add the following liquors:
- 2/3 cup Grand Marnier
- 1/3 cup Gin

Retirement in the Keys
(for the Polley-Clyne crew)

Add lime gelatin mix to 1 cup boiling water. Mix well.

Add the following liquors:
- 1/4 cup Gin
- 1/4 cup Citron Vodka
- 1/4 cup Peach Schnapps
- 1/4 cup Cranberry Liqueur

Retirement in the Outer Banks
(where you'll find the rest of us!)

Add watermelon gelatin mix to 1 cup boiling water.   Mix well.

Add the following liquors:
- 1/4 cup Outer Banks Rum
- 1/4 cup Southern Comfort
- 1/4 cup Peach Schnapps
- 1/4 cup Banana Liqueur

RIFFED   (thanks, Continental!)

Add lemon gelatin mix to 1 cup boiling water.
Mix well.

Add the following liquors:
- 1/2 cup Banana Liqueur
- 1/2 cup Rum

Rock-Around-The-Clock

Add grape gelatin mix to 1 cup boiling water.
Mix well.

Add the following liquors:
- 1/2 cup Gin
- 1/4 cup Blueberry Schapps
- 1/4 cup Cinammon Schnapps

Rusty Nail

Add orange gelatin mix to 1 cup boiling water.
Mix well.

Add the following liquors:
- 1/2 cup Triple Sec
- 1/4 cup Vodka
- 1/4 cup Scotch or Southern Comfort

Sage's Shooter

(this is guaranteed to make you wise beyond your years, or is that ears?   Well, if nothing else, you'll gain a sense of humor........)

Add Hawaiian-pineapple gelatin mix to 1 cup boiling water.   Mix well.

Add the following liquors:
- 1/3 cup Tequila!
- 1/3 cup Coconut Rum!
- 1/3 cup Peach Schnapps!

Sailor's Delight

(for all of those who have the sea in their blood!)

Add cherry gelatin mix to 1 cup boiling water. Mix well.

Add the following liquors:
- 1/2 cup Gin
- 1/4 cup Maraschino or Cherry Liqueur
- 1/4 cup Peach Schnapps

Remember, you can't change the strength or the direction of the winds, but you can set your sails any way you want!

Scarlett O'Hara
(also known as Gone-With-the-Wind)

Add raspberry gelatin mix to 1 cup boiling water. Mix well.

Add the following liquors:
* 2/3 cup Southern Comfort
* 1/3 cup Cranberry Liqueur

Screw Driver

Add orange gelatin mix to 1 cup boiling water. Mix well.

Add the following liquors:
* 3/4 cup Vodka
* 1/4 cup Triple Sec

Seminole
(for those Florida State Fans!!!!!)

Add strawberry gelatin mix to 1 cup boiling water. Mix well.

Add the following liquors:
* 1/2 cup Cinnamon Schnapps
* 1/2 cup Rum

Serendipity
("making valuable discoveries by accident")

Add mixed fruit gelatin mix to 1 cup boiling water.   Mix well.

Add the following liquors:
- 1/2 cup Peach Schnapps
- 1/2 cup Outer Banks Rum

Sex on the Beach

Add Hawaiian-pineapple gelatin mix to 1 cup boiling water.   Mix well.

Add the following liquors:
- 1/3 cup Midori
- 1/3 cup Chambord
- 1/3 cup Vodka

("........been there, ...done that")

Shamrock
(For the Brockes and Waltons!

Add lime gelatin mix to 1 cup boiling water. Mix well.

Add the following liquors:
- 1/2 cup Irish Whiskey
- 1/2 cup Midori

Shark Shooter
(Note, Buffett's Fin song while doing these!)

Add grape gelatin mix to 1 cup boiling water. Mix well.

Add the following liquors:
- 1/2 cup Gin
- 1/4 cup Triple Sec
- 1/4 cup Cinnamon Schnapps

Skinny Dipper
(watch out for the full moon!)

Add blueberry gelatin mix to 1 cup boiling water. Mix well.

Add the following liquors:
- 1/2 cup Coconut Rum
- 1/4 cup Blueberry Schnapps
- 1/4 cup Vodka

Slow Gin Fuzz

Add cherry gelatin mix to 1 cup boiling water. Mix well.

Add the following liquors:
- 1/4 cup Peach Schnapps
- 1/4 cup Sloe Gin
- 1/2 cup Gin

Snow Plow
(For beginners - stay on the Green Slopes!!!)

Add lime gelatin mix to 1 cup boiling water. Mix well.

Add the following liquors:
- 1/2 cup Melon Liquor
- 1/2 cup Triple Sec

Snowshoe
(this is great when you're on Ski Trips in West Virginia, especially if you're in the Hamrick lodge!)

Add lime gelatin mix to 1 cup boiling water. Mix well.

Add the following liquors:
- 1/4 cup Peppermint Schnapps
- 1/4 cup Triple Sec
- 1/2 cup Southern Comfort

South-of-the-Border

Add mixed fruit gelatin mix to 1 cup boiling water. Mix well.

Add the following liquors:
- 1/2 cup Southern Comfort
- 1/2 cup Cherry Liqueur

Spikin' Blues
(Our Volleyball team's special recipe)

Add blueberry gelatin mix to 1 cup boiling water.   Mix well.

Add the following liquors:
- 1/4 cup Blue Curacao
- 1/4 cup Triple Sec
- 1/2 cup Gin

Spin-the-Bottle

Add watermelon gelatin mix to 1 cup boiling water.   Mix well.

Add the following liquors:
- 1/5 cup Tequila
- 1/5 cup Rum
- 1/5 cup Gin
- 1/5 cup Vodka
- 1/5 cup Banana Liqueur

Strawberry Margarita

Add strawberry gelatin mix to 1 cup boiling water.   Mix well.

Add the following liquors:
- 1/2 cup Triple Sec
- 1/2 cup Tequila

Summer Iced-Tea

Add lime gelatin mix to 1 cup boiling water. Mix well.   Add one drop of red food coloring to make it brown!
Add the following liquors:
- 1/4 cup Vodka
- 1/4 cup Gin
- 1/4 cup Rum
- 1/4 cup Triple Sec

(so it doesn't really taste like Iced-Tea.....summ'er meant to,   summ'er not!)

Sunny-Side-Up

Add orange gelatin mix to 1 cup boiling water. Mix well.

Add the following liquors:
- 1/2 cup Citron Vodka
- 1/2 cup Cherry Liqueur

Sunrise

Add lemon gelatin mix to 1 cup boiling water. Mix well.

Add the following liquors:
- 1/2 cup Tequila
- 1/2 cup Apricot Brandy

Sunset

Add cherry gelatin mix to 1 cup boiling water. Mix well.

Add the following liquors:
- 1/2 cup Vodka
- 1/4 cup Banana Liqueur
- 1/4 cup Raspberry Schnapps

Sweet Tart

Add lime gelatin mix to 1 cup boiling water. Mix well.

Add the following liquors:
- 1/4 cup Rum
- 3/4 cup Chambord

Tahiti Punch

Add Hawaiian-pineapple gelatin mix to 1 cup boiling water. Mix well.

Add the following liquors:
- 1/2 cup Spiced Rum
- 1/2 cup Peach Schnapps

Teaser
(for Joe-man and his bar games!)

Add grape gelatin mix to 1 cup boiling water. Mix well.

Add the following liquors:
- 1/4 cup Blueberry Schnapps
- 3/4 cup Vodka

Tee-Time
(this could be anytime for some people I know....)

Add mixed fruit gelatin mix to 1 cup boiling water. Mix well.

Add the following liquors:
- 1/4 cup Tequila
- 3/4 cup Triple Sec

(A guaranteed "hole-in-one")

Temptation

Add Cranberry gelatin mix to 1 cup boiling water. Mix well.

Add the following liquors:
- 1/2 cup Apricot Brandy
- 1/2 cup Midori

Tequila Sunrise

Add orange gelatin mix to 1 cup boiling water. Mix well.

Add the following liquors:
- 1/2 cup Tequila
- 1/2 cup Orange or Cherry Liqueur

Add a drop of grenadine before putting the lid on!!

Tidy-Bowl

Add blueberry gelatin mix to 1 cup boiling water. Mix well.

Add the following liquors:
- 1/2 cup Blue Curacao
- 1/2 cup Vodka

Tornado
(watch out for those funnel clouds!   Or is that just the swirl of water in the toilet....?)

Add lime gelatin mix to 1 cup boiling water. Mix well.

Add the following liquors:
- 1/4 cup Whiskey
- 1/4 cup Vodka
- 1/2 cup Blueberry Schnapps

Transfusion-1

Add blueberry gelatin mix to 1 cup boiling water. Mix well.

Add the following liquors:
- 1/4 cup Vodka
- 1/4 cup Triple Sec
- 1/2 cup Blueberry Schnapps

Transfusion-2

Add grape gelatin mix to 1 cup boiling water. Mix well.

Add the following liquors:
- 1/4 cup Vodka
- 1/4 cup Triple Sec
- 1/2 cup Peach Schnapps

U, V, X, Y, Z (yep, Virgin is in here!)

Ultimate SCHNooter

Add orange gelatin mix to 1 cup boiling water. Mix well.

Add the following liquors:
* 1/4 cup Cinnamon Schnapps
* 1/4 cup Peach Schnapps
* 1/4 cup Raspberry Schnapps
* 1/4 cup Blueberry Schnapps

Unconsciousness

Add blueberry gelatin mix to 1 cup boiling water. Mix well.

Add the following liquors:
* 1/2 cup Vodka
* 1/2 cup Grand Marnier

Underwear Launch

Add mixed fruit gelatin mix to 1 cup boiling water. Mix well.

Add the following liquors:
* 1/2 cup Vodka
* 1/2 cup Kahlua

Virgin

Add <u>ANY flavor</u> Gelatin Mix to 1 cup boiling water.   Mix well.

Add the following liquids:
- 1/2 cup pineapple or apple Juice
- 1/2 cup cold water

(Kids like this one too!   Just be sure not to mix them up with the "big-kid" shooters!!)

Virtual Reality

Add blueberry gelatin mix to 1 cup boiling water.   Mix well.

Add the following liquors:
- 1/4 cup Blue Curacao
- 1/4 cup Vodka
- 1/2 cup Peppermint Schnapps

Often known as an upper-management drink.

Viva La Difference!

Add Cranberry gelatin mix to 1 cup boiling water.   Mix well.

Add the following liquor:
- 1 cup Sloe Gin

Watermelon

Add watermelon gelatin mix to 1 cup boiling water. Mix well.

Add the following liquors:
- 1/4 cup Midori
- 1/4 cup Peach Schnapps
- 1/2 cup Rum

Spit out the seeds, not the shooter!

Wedded Bliss!!
(for the Morris', Pittard's, and Edwards' nuptials - 1994!!)

Add mixed fruit gelatin mix to 1 cup boiling water. Mix well.

Add the following liquors:
- 1/4 cup Tequila (for the Morris's)
- 1/4 cup Vodka (for the Edward's)
- 1/4 cup Wild Turkey (for the Pittard's)
- 1/4 cup Peach Schnapps
                     (for the heck of it)

Whale Tail

Add lime gelatin mix to 1 cup boiling water. Mix well.

Add the following liquors:
- 1/2 cup Blue Curacao
- 1/2 cup Dark Rum

Whaley's Whine
(or "can I drive, please!!?")

Add Cranberry gelatin mix to 1 cup boiling water. Mix well.

Add the following liquors:
- 1/2 cup Rum
- 1/4 cup Cranberry Liqueur
- 1/4 cup Peach Schnapps

Whiskey Sour

Add lemon gelatin mix to 1 cup boiling water. Mix well.

Add the following liquors:
- 1/2 cup Whiskey
- 1/2 cup Triple Sec

X-Ray

Add lime gelatin mix to 1 cup boiling water.
Mix well.

Add the following liquors:
- 1/2 cup Southern Comfort
- 1/4 cup Cinnamon Schnapps
- 1/4 cup Peppermint Schnapps

YABADABADO
(for us kids growing up with the Flintstones!)

Add grape gelatin mix to 1 cup boiling water.
Mix well.

Add the following liquors:
- 1/2 cup **B**anana Liqueur (for Bam Bam!)
- 1/2 cup **P**each Schnapps (for Pebbles!)

Yankee-Doodle-Dandy

Add Hawaiian-pineapple gelatin mix to 1 cup
boiling water.   Mix well.

Add the following liquors:
- 1/2 cup Orange Curacao
- 1/4 cup Light Rum
- 1/4 cup Southern Comfort

Yellow Pigeon
(Except for the color, you could also call this a White Dove!)

Add lemon gelatin mix to 1 cup boiling water. Mix well.

Add the following liquors:
- 1/2 cup White Rum
- 1/2 cup Anisette or Sambuca

YES, I AM
(Make sure you nod your head slowly, saying "yes, I am..!" to any question asked while eating this shooter)

Add orange gelatin mix to 1 cup boiling water. Mix well.

Add the following liquors:
- 1/4 cup Orange Vodka
- 1/4 cup Triple Sec
- 1/2 cup Orange Curacao

ZAP

Add lime gelatin mix to 1 cup boiling water. Mix well.

Add the following liquors:
- 1/4 cup Margarita Schnapps
- 1/4 cup Triple Sec
- 1/2 cup Cuervo Gold

Zombie

Add Hawaiian-pineapple gelatin mix to 1 cup boiling water. Mix well.

Add the following liquors:
- 1/4 cup Light Rum
- 1/4 cup Dark Rum
- 1/4 cup Coconut Rum
- 1/4 cup Banana Liqueur

ZOOM
(RMC and Beach Party Games)

Add raspberry gelatin mix to 1 cup boiling water. Mix well.

Add the following liquors:
- 1/2 cup Courant Vodka
- 1/4 cup Light Rum
- 1/4 cup Cinnamon Schnapps

V. PARTY SUGGESTIONS

Most of the gelatin-shooters will be the color
of the gelatin that you use. In some cases, you
may want to change or enhance the color of
the gelatin by adding a drop or two of food
coloring to the batch before you pour it into
the cups.

For Washington Redskin football game parties,
you may want to serve shooters that have
Maroon and Gold colors (any of the raspberry
or cherry shooters and orange shooters).

For games against the Dallas Cowboys, use any
of the blue shooters (Blue Hawaii, Tidy Bowl,
etc.).

For Jimmy Buffett concerts, our beach people
generally pack a cooler full of Margarita's,
Piña Colada's, Bahama Mama's, Sex on the
Beach, and Shark Shooters.

For any of the sporting events (Olympics,
World Series, Super Bowl, Citrus Bowl, once a
year sex, etc.) choose the colors from your
favorite team playing, or even both teams,
and make the shooters based on those colors.

For holidays, make shooters in the predominant holiday color:

Flag Day or Fourth of July: Red and Blue Shooters - add a dab of whipped cream to each before you put on the top to get the "white".

St. Patricks Day: Try the Shamrock, or any of the green shooters!

Christmas: Green and Red shooters, or add Goldwasser (liqueur with gold specs) in place of any of the liqueurs in the recipe.

Cinco de Mayo: Margarita Shooters of course!

Octoberfest: Red, Yellow, and Dark Brown shooters - the colors of the Deutch Flag!

Weddings are also an appropriate time to bring shooters!!   If your wedding friends are having a contemporary wedding, they can feed shooters to each other instead of the traditional wedding cake.   And they make lovely table decorations for the wedding party! Use the shooters that ask for Goldwasser for that extra special touch.

Besides choosing gelatin-shooters for your party favors, they also make great **games**!

Most of us keep <u>Twister</u> in our game closets. Make shooters the color of the circles (red, blue, green, yellow). You can place them on the circles or leave it up to the spinner to distribute - when a player must put a foot on a colored circle, the player is also fed the appropriate color shooter! Players tend to fall quicker during this version of the game!

Another fun game is <u>Gelatin-shooter Toss</u>. Each player has a partner. They each have two shooters in their possession. They stand three feet apart. One partner removes the first shooter (preferably using the finger method...) and tosses it towards the partner's mouth (which should be open at this point). Then the receiving partner gets to throw the shooter. Then the partners should be positioned six feet apart and repeat the tosses. Whichever team catches (and swallows) the most shooters wins! Note, this one should not be played in formal attire, or in newly carpeted homes.

You get the idea!! Go for it, be creative, and always encourage designated drivers (It's not considered safe to eat shooters while you drive unless your tongue is extremely long!!!)